ENGAGEMENT

31-DAY DEVOTIONALS FOR LIFE

A Series

DEEPAK REJU
Series Editor

ENGAGEMENT

PREPARING
FOR
MARRIAGE

MIKE McKINLEY

P&R
PUBLISHING

P.O. BOX 817 • PHILLIPSBURG • NEW JERSEY 08865-0817

Printed in the United States of America

Library of Congress Cataloging-in-Publication Data

Names: McKinley, Mike, 1975- author.
Title: Engagement : preparing for marriage / Mike McKinley.
Description: Phillipsburg, New Jersey : P&R Publishing, 2020. | Series: 31-day devotionals for life | Summary: "How will God's gospel love be displayed as you get ready for marriage? Take a month to prepare your heart using thoughtful devotional readings, reflection questions, and practical action points"-- Provided by publisher.
Identifiers: LCCN 2019058507 | ISBN 9781629954943 (paperback) | ISBN 9781629954950 (epub) | ISBN 9781629954967 (mobi)
Subjects: LCSH: Marriage--Religious aspects--Christianity. | Betrothal--Religious aspects--Christianity. | Couples--Prayers and devotions.
Classification: LCC BV835 .M3426 2020 | DDC 242/.644--dc23
LC record available at https://lccn.loc.gov/2019058507

For Jon Cornish,
with the prayerful hope that this will serve
you well in your future marriage

Contents

Tips for Reading This Devotional

EARLY IN OUR MARRIAGE, my wife and I lived on the top floor of a town house, in a small one-bedroom apartment. Whenever it rained, leaks in the roof would drip through the ceiling and onto our floors. I remember placing buckets in different parts of the apartment and watching the water slowly drip, one drop at a time. I put large buckets out and thought, *It'll take a while to fill them.* The water built up over time, and often I was surprised at how quickly those buckets filled up, overflowing if I didn't pay close enough attention.

Like rain filling up a bucket, this devotional will surprise you. It may not seem like much; just a few verses every day. Drip. Drip. Drip. Yet a few drops of Scripture daily can satiate your parched soul. The transformative power of these readings will build over time and overflow into your life.

Why does a book like this make such a difference?

We start with Scripture. God's Word is powerful. Used by the Holy Spirit, it turns the hearts of kings, brings comfort to the lowly, and gives spiritual sight to the blind. It transforms lives and turns them upside down. We know that the Bible is God's very own words, so we read and study it to know God himself.

Our study of Scripture is practical. Theology should change how we live. It's crucial to connect the Word with your struggles. Often, as you read this devotional, you'll see the word *you* because Mike speaks directly to you, the reader. Each reading contains at least one reflection question and practical suggestion. You'll get much more from this experience if you answer the questions and do the practical exercises. Don't skip them. Do them for the sake of your own soul.

Our study of Scripture is worshipful. As you study your Bible, you will learn that marriage is all about God. The Lord makes a covenant with his people and shows us what faithfulness and commitment look like. He demonstrates his love by sending Jesus to die for our sins and by not holding our sins against us. As Scripture teaches us about God's relationship with his people, it helps to prepare us for the lifelong commitment of marriage. If God is faithful, loving, forgiving, and enduring in the commitment he has made with us, so also should we be toward our fiancés if we call ourselves Christians. As we gaze at God and the gospel, they will teach us much about marriage and inspire us to greater worship.

If you find this devotional helpful (and I trust that you will!), reread it in different seasons of your life. It will help you to get prepared for marriage, but you'll find that many of Mike's meditations will be encouraging to you as a married couple as well. So work through it this coming month, and then come back to it a year from now, to remind yourself about what God and the gospel teach us about marriage. You'll also find additional resources at the end of the book to help you as you continue your journey.

That's enough for now. Let's begin.

Deepak Reju

Introduction

SOMEONE ONCE SAID that wisdom is not learning from your mistakes; it is learning from the mistakes of others.

That sentiment should give you a sense of the qualifications I have to write this little book. I have been married to Karen, my college sweetheart, for more than twenty years. In addition to that, in my capacity as a pastor I have walked with couples at every stage of the marriage relationship—from engagement to widowhood and practically all that fall between the two. As a result of those experiences, I have made (or seen other people make) pretty much every marriage mistake imaginable. My hope is to put some of those experiences to work for your benefit. Perhaps you can stand on my shoulders, and the shoulders of the people I know, and avoid our mistakes!

With all that said, however, the most important thing that you can do for your upcoming marriage is *not* to learn tips and skills that will make you more prepared for a life of matrimonial bliss. In fact, that approach to premarital preparation underlies a lot of the reasons that couples struggle. Fundamentally, your marriage is not about you and your spouse. It is not merely the sum of your communication skills, sexual intimacy, and ability to bridge whatever gaps may exist between your view of the world and your spouse's. Those "horizontal" factors are certainly important, but they are not what is *most* important.

God tells us in his Word that he created marriage to be a demonstration of his own love and character—to show his own incredible love for his people. Marriage is intended to be both a sign of God's love and also a reminder that, at the end of the age, God's people will be given as a bride to their bridegroom—the Lord Jesus Christ. This is the most important thing you can know about marriage. Because of that, we will spend a lot of time (especially at the beginning of this devotional) talking about what marriage tells us about God and about ourselves. Though it may not sound very practical, I am convinced that the reason many couples struggle is because one or both of the people in them lose sight of the "vertical" focus that God intended for their marriage. It is that focus that should guide all our decisions and actions.

Let's suppose that a husband and wife have a conflict. Maybe you and your fiancé have already experienced a few of those, and so you can call an example to mind. Or perhaps it is difficult for you to imagine ever fighting, besotted with moony engagement bliss as you may well be. If that is you, congratulations! But you can be sure that the day is coming; any healthy relationship between married sinners is going to have to deal with some conflict eventually.

So let's say that our newlyweds are having an argument over their finances or where they should spend their Christmas vacation. The conviction that underlies this devotional is that what this couple needs, first and foremost, is not better anger management techniques or a system to split up the holidays fairly but rather an understanding that God has created their marriage for a definite purpose. As a result, both husband and wife are under a type of constraint—they are not free to do whatever they wish or to pursue their own desires at all costs. Their Creator has given them to each other to be a picture of his love and forgiveness. The way that they treat each other, even in times of conflict and stress, is meant to mirror the self-giving love that exists between Christ and his church.

That conviction, if allowed to take root deep in our hearts, will do more to build healthy, happy, and God-glorifying marriages than a thousand lessons on how men and women communicate differently. There is a place for advice on communication (and on other aspects of marriage), and indeed we will get to those kinds of things in this devotional. But if those lessons are not grounded on the foundation of God's purposes for marriage, they will crumble like sandcastles into the sea.

Before we begin, one more piece of housekeeping is in order. To put all my cards on the table, I want you to know that I write this devotional with a few assumptions in mind.

- I assume that you are preparing yourself for an upcoming marriage. If that does not fit your exact circumstances, you are still welcome to read on; in fact, I hope that you do. But my intention is to calibrate my illustrations and applications to someone who is about to get married.
- I hope that you and your intended are engaged in premarital counseling through your local church. This devotional is not meant to replace that crucial piece of your joint preparation for marriage. I am writing to you as an individual to help you to prepare *yourself* for marriage rather than writing to both of you as a couple.
- I assume that you are a Christian. If you are not, then again, you are more than welcome to read on. But I will write as if you believe that the Bible is true and you wish to bring your thoughts and life and marriage into an ever closer alignment with the things that are revealed to us within it.

I write this with prayers that the Lord might use it in some small way in your life and marriage, for his glory and for your happiness!

THE BIG PICTURE
OF MARRIAGE

DAY 1

God Is . . . a Husband?

"For your Maker is your husband, the LORD of hosts is his name; and the Holy One of Israel is your Redeemer, the God of the whole earth he is called. For the LORD has called you like a wife." (Isa. 54:5–6)

WHEN YOU THINK about what God is like, what comes to your mind?

This is a difficult question. After all, how can limited people understand an infinite being? How can created beings comprehend what it would be like to have always existed? What does it mean for sinful people who are living in a fallen world to think well about a perfectly Holy One?

Because he is gracious, God wants to be known by the people he has created; and to that end he has stooped down to reveal himself to us. In the Bible, the Lord uses many metaphors and word pictures to help us to understand what he is like and how he relates to us. He is a King, because he rules over us and is a lawgiver (see Ps. 47). He is a Judge, in that he is the one who evaluates all our thoughts and actions (see Ps. 7:11). He is a Shepherd, for he leads his people to safety and provision (see Ps. 23).

But perhaps the most surprising and revealing image that God uses for himself in Scripture is that of a husband to his people. When God says through the prophet Isaiah that he is our husband and his people are his wife, it is a picture of the most intimate kind of knowledge and love. We know how a husband feels about his wife, and we might be tempted to wonder whether or not God, the "Holy One" and "Redeemer," could really love his people like that. The answer, gloriously, is yes!

The fact that God refers to himself as a husband tells us something important about him and the amazing love that he has for us, but it also shows us something very important about the institution of marriage. If God is a husband, then marriage is not merely a social construct or even primarily a way for people to find companionship and start a family. Instead, marriage is fundamentally a picture of God's love. It is a way for us to understand and display the depth and intensity of the love God has for his people.

In the end, the thing that makes a marriage a Christian marriage is not that the couple attend church together (though they should) or raise their children to know the gospel (though that is a good thing to do). At its essence, a Christian marriage should be a man and a woman who understand that they have been brought together into an intimate relationship for the purpose of learning and displaying the way that God loves us in Christ. This is a foundational truth on which to build your own marriage.

Reflect: Take time to meditate on the truth that God, as your husband, knows you intimately and loves you—even if you do not always feel like he does. How might a better understanding of God's love help you to love your future spouse?

Act: Find a Christian who has been married for a while and ask them how marriage has helped them to better understand God's love.

DAY 2

An Unfaithful Bride

*"How sick is your heart, declares the Lord GOD, because you did . . .
the deeds of a brazen prostitute. . . . Adulterous wife, who receives
strangers instead of her husband! Men give gifts to all prostitutes,
but you gave your gifts to all your lovers, bribing them to come to
you from every side with your whorings." (Ezek. 16:30, 32–33)*

LATE LAST NIGHT, I received an email from a couple who
were asking to meet with me for some marriage counseling. It's
typical for such emails to come in after I have gone to bed. I guess
that by the time a couple puts kids to bed, has a vigorous fight,
and calms down enough to conclude that they should get some
help, it is going to be pretty late in the evening!

What made this email remarkable is that the person who sent
it to me admitted that they had been unfaithful to their spouse.
Being a pastor means helping people through these kinds of situations, and sadly I have had to deal with this issue before. But even
so, the news made me feel sick. I remembered the couple meet-
ing with me for premarital counseling; I remembered the joy and
beauty of their wedding ceremony. Now, their immediate future
will involve wading through intense feelings of anger and betrayal.

Today's shocking passage from the prophet Ezekiel is not one
that you normally read in a book aimed at preparing couples for
marriage. But, just as we saw in yesterday's reading that marriage
teaches us about the spiritual reality of God's love, in a similar way
this passage is one of the places where the Bible uses marriage to
vividly illustrate the nature of our sin.

And it is remarkable that when God wants us to understand
our sin, he uses adultery as his illustration. God is the husband
of his people, but the citizens of Jerusalem in Ezekiel's day were

like an unfaithful wife. They were promiscuous in their worship of other gods, and so they are pictured here as a woman who joyfully receives multiple lovers. You and I may not be guilty of the specific sins that tempted people in those days, but whenever we look to sin to give us the joy and satisfaction that God promises us, we are throwing our lot in with them.

What does that mean for us? If marriage is meant to teach us about our relationship to God, then we should sit and contemplate seriously the idea that our sin is like spiritual adultery. It is unfaithfulness to and betrayal of God, our husband. Imagine how terrible it would feel if your upcoming marriage were marked by infidelity and betrayal—and let that feeling help you to hate your sin and be quick to repent when you do sin. Do not take sin lightly, for God does not take it lightly.

Reflect: Are there areas in your life in which you have taken sin lightly? Remember that God takes sin so seriously that it cost him his Son to restore us.

Act: Repent and ask for God's forgiveness and for the strength to resist sin—particularly in your upcoming marriage.

DAY 3

A Restored Bride

*"I will build a wall against her, so that she cannot find her
paths. She shall pursue her lovers but not overtake them. . . .
Then she shall say, 'I will go and return to my first husband,
for it was better for me then than now.'" (Hosea 2:6–7)*

*"I will betroth you to me in righteousness and in justice,
in steadfast love and in mercy. I will betroth you to me in
faithfulness. And you shall know the* Lord.*" (Hosea 2:19–20)*

THE BEGINNING OF the book of Hosea provides a real-
life parable that helps us to understand God's faithful love. The
Lord instructs the prophet to marry a prostitute named Gomer;
even though Hosea cared for her and provided for her, she was
always looking to other lovers. The idea seems to be that Gomer's
unfaithfulness was a picture of Israel's sinful idolatry against the
Lord. Hosea and Gomer's marriage was a picture of the truth that
we saw in our previous devotional: that sin is spiritual adultery.

Now, we might expect that the point of this parable was to
make an example of this unfaithful woman—to give her what she
deserved for her sins and thus to show Israel the consequences of
idolatry. But it turns out that this is not a story about judgment; it
is a story about redemption. Through the prophet, the Lord says
that he will intervene in two ways to deliver his people out of the
midst of their rebellion.

First, he would make their experience of idolatry difficult and
unfulfilling—would "build a wall against her, so that she [could]
not find . . . her lovers" (see Hos. 2:6–7). The plan was that Israel's
disappointment with their sin, and with their failure to find what
they were looking for in other gods, would cause them to return
to the Lord.

The second promise amounts to an astounding word of grace: God would establish a renewed "betrothal." Betrothal is like a more formal version of our idea of "engagement" and is established when the would-be groom pays a price and gives gifts to the father of the would-be bride. In this case, the Lord would reestablish his relationship with his wayward people through the gifts of righteousness, justice, steadfast love, mercy, and faithfulness (see v. 19). They would be spiritually transformed and restored to a personal relationship with their God (see v. 20).

Now, you might be wondering to yourself, what on earth does this have to do with my engagement and upcoming marriage?

Do you remember when we said that marriage is meant to be a picture of God's love (see day 1)? Here in Hosea 2 we get an amazing glimpse into exactly what that love is like. God's love is not the love a groom has for his bride when she looks radiant and beautiful on their wedding day. Nor is it the delight that a bride feels when she sees the groom looking dashing in his tuxedo. The Lord's love is much greater than the love of this "honeymoon stage."

The picture of his love that we see in Hosea 2 is extraordinary—it is an underserved love, an undying love, a purifying love. It is a love that will ultimately find its fulfillment in Jesus.

Reflect: God does not love you because of how good you are. He loves you despite your sins.

Act: Make a list of three ways you might be called upon to show love in your future marriage. Are you committed to showing love even if your spouse does not deserve it?

DAY 4

The True Bridegroom

"I said, 'I am not the Christ, but I have been sent before him.'
The one who has the bride is the bridegroom. The friend of the
bridegroom, who stands and hears him, rejoices greatly at the
bridegroom's voice. Therefore this joy of mine is now complete.
He must increase, but I must decrease." (John 3:28–30)

IT MAY BE that the previous days' readings have left you feeling
a bit of a tension. We have seen that God loves his people with
the passionate love of a husband. That's all well and good. What is
more difficult for us to understand is how God can be committed
to loving unfaithful (meaning spiritually adulterous!) people like
us. How can he pledge his love to sinners?

The words in today's verses come from John the Baptist, and
in them we begin to see how God is going to resolve this tension. It
is not insignificant that John refers to Jesus as "the bridegroom"—
he would have been well aware of the significance of that term in
the Old Testament. When he calls Jesus the bridegroom, John is
saying that he is the fulfillment of everything that the prophets
said God would be to his people. Jesus is God in the flesh; he is
here to love us with a passionate, purifying love.

As God's revelation progresses throughout the pages of Scripture, we get an ever clearer picture of just what his love looks
like. It looks just like Jesus! Jesus came to teach us about God's
love through his preaching and parables (see, for example, Luke
15:20). He came to broadcast God's love through his mercy and
miracles (see, for example, Matt. 14:14). He came to provide the
ultimate demonstration of God's love through his sacrificial death
for our sins (see Rom. 5:8). On the cross, Jesus stood in our place
and took the consequences for all our spiritual unfaithfulness. He

died under the anger of God so that we could always be treated as a faithful and pure bride. Jesus's love is the love that God spoke of in Hosea 2—the love of a husband for a bride who has been unfaithful and poisoned by sin; a love that has the power to transform and remake its object.

So while we have already said that marriage is all about God's love, now we are ready to be more specific: marriage is all about God's love being shown to sinful people in Jesus.

Jesus's death and resurrection convince us that God loves us—they are the ultimate proof that God cares about us and wants us to be with him for eternity (see John 3:16).

Reflecting on God's love might not seem like an urgent priority for you as you prepare for your marriage, but it is. If you are not sure of God's love, then you will always be looking to your spouse to fill up that hole in your soul. And I can promise you that your future spouse is not equipped and designed for that work! In fact, few things will choke the life out of a marriage more quickly than two people who are looking to each other to provide the sense of ultimate love and security that only God can give us.

Reflect: Do you believe that God loves you? How can you cultivate a greater sense of his love for you in Jesus?

Act: Think of ways that you might be tempted to look to your spouse for the ultimate security, purpose, and love that only God can give. What can you put in place in your relationship to help you to avoid that situation?

DAY 5

A Wedding at the End of Time

I heard what seemed to be the voice of a great multitude . . . crying out, "Hallelujah! . . . The marriage of the Lamb has come, and his Bride has made herself ready; it was granted her to clothe herself with fine linen, bright and pure." . . . And the angel said to me, ". . . Blessed are those who are invited to the marriage supper of the Lamb." (Rev. 19:6–9)

AS A PASTOR, I enjoy officiating at weddings (well, except for the outdoor weddings in August—those are terrible!). There is always a palpable sense of joy and excitement as the bride and groom and the people they love gather to celebrate the gift of marriage.

But as great as wedding ceremonies are, people seem to enjoy the receptions afterward even more. A good wedding reception includes some of the most pleasant things in life—family, friends, good food, good drink, and your seventy-year-old aunt dancing to the Jackson 5 (okay, maybe not that last part). And at its heart, the joy of a wedding reception is rooted both in the past (in loving relationships that have been established) and also in the future that we imagine for the happy couple (which involves things like a wonderful life together, a home, and children).

In light of that, the book of Revelation tells us that history will find its culmination in a great wedding feast (cf. Isa. 25:6–9). On that day, the people of God will be clothed in beautiful, bright linens, and the Lamb (Jesus) will take them to be his bride. There will be joy and exultation, followed by a celebration.

Here's the picture that is being painted for us: right now, we do not live in the physical presence of Jesus, but a day is coming when Jesus and his people will be together for all eternity. And on that day, there is going to be a party—a great celebration of all that Jesus has done for us in the past and of all that this means for our future.

That future reality should impact the way that we live today and plan for tomorrow. You can be sure that your marriage will have troubles. Two sinners living together in a fallen world with bodies that will age and deteriorate—that's a recipe for some difficulties!

But if you are a Christian, your story has a 100 percent chance of having a happy ending. That means that your best days and your greatest joys will not be experienced in this life. Your upcoming marriage will not be your only, your best, or your most lasting source of happiness.

Reflect: How would someone who is sure that they will spend their eternal life joyfully in the presence of God make decisions differently from someone who is living as if all the joy they will ever get comes in this life? How does that impact the way that you think about trials you may face in your upcoming marriage?

Act: Take note of the things that happen today that are disappointing, frustrating, or painful. Then think about how you will feel about those things on the day of the great "marriage supper of the Lamb." Let the difficult things in your life today help you to look forward to that day.

DAY 6

Jesus's Marriage and Yours

Now as the church submits to Christ, so also wives should submit in everything to their husbands. Husbands, love your wives, as Christ loved the church and gave himself up for her. . . . This mystery is profound, and I am saying that it refers to Christ and the church. (Eph. 5:24–25, 32)

AS WE HAVE already seen, marriage is a significant motif in the Bible—in the Old Testament, God speaks of himself as Israel's husband and Israel as his faithless bride. Expanding on that idea, Jesus is referred to as "the bridegroom" and the church as his bride (see 2 Cor. 11:2).

As you contemplate your soon-to-be marriage, consider this: which came first—God's love or the institution of marriage? Do you think God looked around for something that would serve as a helpful metaphor for his intimate love for his people and decided that marriage was his best choice? Or do you think that the very reason he created marriage in the first place was so that it could serve as a display of his love?

Paul's words in Ephesians 5 make it clear that the latter is the case. God designed marriage for the express purpose of displaying his character and love. A husband is not supposed to merely love his wife in a vague, sentimental sense. He is supposed to love her in a specific way that follows a specific pattern—to love her "as Christ loved the church" (v. 25). And a wife is to respond to her husband's love in the same way that the church responds to the love of Christ (see v. 24).

The problem is that we tend to view marriage very differently from this. Most of us naturally think of marriage as a way for us to get our needs met while we meet our spouses' needs. So even in our choice of whom to marry, we might instinctively look for the "best catch" we can possibly get. We want someone who is pretty enough, smart enough, funny enough, and financially secure—and all those things are fine. But the Bible rarely talks about marriage in terms of how much we enjoy it or what we get out of it. Instead, God's Word focuses on the obligations that we have in our marriages—namely, to show love to our spouses.

Hopefully your marriage will be marked by joy, pleasure, fun, and excitement. But those things are not the final goal. The goal of your marriage is for you and your spouse to reflect the love of God in the way that you love each other. Think about how that might look:

- When you tell your children about the gracious, generous, forgiving, intimate love of God for his people, you want them to think to themselves, "I've seen that kind of love before. That's how Mom and Dad love each other."
- When your unbelieving friends see your marriage, they should observe a kind of care, honor, and sacrifice that surprises them. When they comment on it, you can tell them that such love comes from Jesus, who loved his people to the point of death on a cross.

Reflect: Have you ever seen a Christian marriage that seemed to reflect God's love? What about that marriage stands out to you?

Act: Make a list of a few things over which you and your fiancé might have conflict. Talk together about how your approach to those subjects might reflect a selfish mindset (one that is focused on getting your needs met) rather than a God-centered one.

DAY 7

The Enemy of Marriage

Be sober-minded; be watchful. Your adversary the devil prowls around like a roaring lion, seeking someone to devour. (1 Peter 5:8)

MARRIAGE IS MEANT to be a living picture of the intimate love of God for his people. It should come as no surprise, then, that the devil hates marriage and seeks to undermine it. Satan despises whatever glorifies God, so he entices husbands and wives to exhibit behaviors that paint a false picture of God's love. To borrow Peter's phrasing, the devil prowls around Christian marriages like a lion, looking for couples to devour.

If you look at Scripture, you will see that the Evil One seems to use the same strategies over and over again. These include the following.

Temptation. Sin works against the health of marriages. Sometimes patterns of sin develop imperceptibly over time, and a couple can settle into long-term habits of bitterness, anger, and resentment without even realizing it. Other sins, like sexual immorality, are more obvious. The devil doesn't care which sins cripple your marriage, just as long as something does.

Deception. The devil is a liar and the father of lies (see John 8:44). Think about the lies our world believes about marriage: It is unnecessary (why not just live together?). It cramps your style (the old "ball and chain"). It can be dissolved when either party feels that it is no longer enjoyable (quickie no-fault divorce!). If you ever find yourself tempted by these thoughts, you can be sure that the devil is prowling.

Physical attacks. The devil is a murderer (see John 8:44). So it should come as no surprise when the Bible tells us that some physical suffering is a form of Satanic oppression (see, for example,

Luke 13:11). To the devil's delight, many marriages crumble in the face of illness, weakness, pain, and loss.

That might sound frightening—but there is good news! Jesus is more powerful than the devil (see 1 John 3:8). Nothing that the devil might do can destroy any of God's people. God has given us his Spirit to help us when the devil prowls around, looking for husbands and wives to devour.

Marriage is a wonderful blessing; but when you take your wedding vows, you enter a spiritual combat zone. Are you preparing for the devil's schemes? Are you readying yourself for the day when the tempter-liar-murderer comes for your marriage?

There are three things that you can do to resist the devil.

Be watchful. Satan thrives when people are not paying attention to him. Pay attention and see where he may be gaining a foothold.

Be prayerful. Prayer is a way of expressing confidence in and dependence on the Lord. You need God's help to combat the devil's schemes, and prayer is one of the avenues through which you receive his help.

Be connected. The antelope that wanders from the herd is the one that the lion picks off first. You need to be connected to other believers in a local church. If you wait until trouble comes and then try to recruit people to be involved in your life, it will not go well. As a pastor, I see a lot of troubled marriages. Almost as a rule, the ones that survive and thrive are the ones involving couples who have established close relationships with others in the church.

Reflect: How might you be tempted to believe lies about marriage?

Act: Pray with your fiancé, asking God to keep you safe from the devil's schemes.

Act: Talk with your fiancé about how you can build relationships with others in the church.

DAY 8

A Potential Idol

Little children, keep yourselves from idols. (1 John 5:21)

WHEN WE THINK about idols, we might conjure up images of people worshipping statues and carved images. And certainly a lot of that goes on in the Bible—from what we see in the Old Testament, it seems that Israel could not quit their love for idol worship. But if we look more closely, we see that the Bible's understanding of what constitutes an idol goes deeper than that. For example, in two different places—Ephesians 5:5 and Colossians 3:5—the apostle Paul equates greed and covetousness with idolatry.

Idolatry is a problem that goes far beyond bowing down to an image. It involves our hearts' deepest longings. Worshipping God requires our full heart, soul, mind, and strength (see Mark 12:30). We look to the true God as the ultimate source of our satisfaction and joy (see Ps. 35:9). But when something other than God captures our hearts—when we are ruled by a coveting, a craving, or a longing for pleasure and joy that come from something other than God—in that moment we are worshipping an idol. So when John ends his first letter with an appeal to the church to "keep yourselves from idols," he is probably not worried about them going to the temple and worshipping a statue. He is warning them against making their own hearts into houses of false worship.

The things that we turn into idols are not always bad things. Oftentimes they are blessings that God has given us but that have gone on to displace him as the object of our deepest love and trust. All the good things in our lives—be they health, beauty, money, children, a good job, or even our marriages—have the potential to serve as a substitute for God in our hearts. In fact, the more wonderful something is, the more dangerous an idol it has the potential to be.

Because marriage is such an amazing gift, when our hearts warp it into an idol, it is a terribly powerful one. Looking to your marriage to provide you with joy, peace, and contentment at the deepest levels of your soul is a recipe for disaster—and for several reasons.

It dishonors God, leading us to make less of him than we ought to. God deserves to be worshipped and adored for who he is and what he has done. Anything that displaces him from the primary position in our hearts is an offense to him.

Idolatry kills marriages. Your spouse is not meant for the task of filling your heart's deepest longings. They will never be able to love you enough, make you feel good enough about yourself, serve you enough, or bring you enough of a purpose for your life. Our hearts are simply too deep; our longings are too intense. You were designed to find all those things first and foremost in God— not in your spouse. Your spouse's love and care and service are meant to be an echo of God's—not a replacement for them. If you insist on looking to your spouse for what God alone can give, you will crush your relationship.

My friend, keep yourself from making marriage an idol!

Reflect: As you think about your relationship with your fiancé and about your future marriage, what are some good things that might threaten to become idols?

Act: Write out a prayer to God in which you commit yourself to putting him first in your heart. Ask the Holy Spirit for the power and wisdom to live that commitment out.

DIFFERENT BY DESIGN

DAY 9

The Same and Different

Then God said, "Let us make man in our image, after our likeness."
... So God created man in his own image, in the image of God he
created him; male and female he created them. (Gen. 1:26–27)

THE CREATION NARRATIVE that we read in Genesis serves
as our introduction to God. We learn that he existed before "the
beginning" (see Gen. 1:1) and that he is a God who speaks (see
Gen. 1:3).

The creation account also hints at a truth about God that is
fleshed out for us in the rest of the Bible. When he speaks about
the creation of humanity, God says, "Let us create man." You can
imagine that centuries of Israelite readers would have puzzled over
that wording—God is one (see Deut. 6:4), so who is the "us"? It
is not until the New Testament that we see clearly what the Old
Testament has been hinting at—the one true God exists eternally
in three persons: the Father, the Son, and the Holy Spirit.

This truth about God's Trinitarian nature is a reality that
stands behind all creation—and especially the institution of
marriage. You do not really see the point of marriage unless you
understand that God is three in one.

The key to understanding this important truth is found in
the words "in our image." When God creates humanity, he makes
people in his image. That means that we are like God in some
ways (are capable of love, creativity, and making moral judg-
ments) and, even more importantly, that we are created to reflect
or demonstrate what God is like.

It makes sense that the one God, who exists eternally in three
persons, would make human beings in his image to be both male
and female. The Father, Son, and Spirit express unity (in that,

35

while each person is fully God, there is only one God) and loving community (in that each person is distinct but loves the others). That idea might make our head hurt, but humanity is created to reflect the image of this God who is both unity and diversity. Men and women are the same—they are human beings made in God's image. But they are also different—they have been created with different roles and identities. When a man and a woman come together in marriage, this union of sameness and distinctness acts as an echo of God's identity. It reflects the image of God.

Most people like the idea that men and women are the same. But our society has grown uncomfortable with the idea that there are deep and important differences between the genders as well. Many think that if we believe that men and women are different, it will necessarily lead us to say that one is better than the other.

The Trinity, however, shows us how persons can be distinct individuals and yet still be equal in terms of their dignity and worth. Marriage reflects something of this amazing reality. When a man and a woman come together, their unity-in-diversity is displayed to the world. There might be occasions when those differences make marriage challenging—unlike the Trinity, husbands and wives aren't always on the same page. But in God's plan, we know it is better that we marry someone who is both like us and unlike us.

Reflect: How is your future spouse different from you? Do you sometimes wish that they were just like you? What would you miss out on if they were just a carbon copy of you and your strengths?

Act: Look for things about your fiancé that reflect God's character—especially in ways that are not your own strengths. Thank God for those things.

DAY 10

Husbands, Love Like Jesus!

Husbands, love your wives, as Christ loved the church
and gave himself up for her. (Eph. 5:25)

IN YESTERDAY'S READING, we laid out a foundational truth—that God intentionally created men and women to be different from each other. Previous generations did not need this to be pointed out to them. You have to work pretty hard to convince yourself that this is not so. Scripture gives us clear instruction about how men and women have different roles and responsibilities. In the next two readings, we will consider the husband's role in a marriage. After that, we will look at the wife's role.

In Ephesians 5:25, Paul tells husbands to love their wives. That may not be all that surprising to you; everyone knows that married people should love each other. But, if you are paying attention, what Paul says next is shocking: husbands are supposed to love their wives "as Christ loved the church." That's quite a standard—husbands are not told to imitate Romeo or some character from a romantic movie; our love is supposed to look like Jesus's love for his church!

How did Jesus love the church? Notice two things.

Jesus's love is specific. Who does Ephesians 5:25 tell us that Jesus loves? His love is for a very specific group: his church—all men and women, in every time and place, who repent of their sin and put their trust in him. Jesus's love is reserved for his bride, the church.

Husbands are called to show their wives that same specific love. Too many people fall for some idealized, unrealistic version of their spouses that doesn't actually exist anywhere outside their minds. But a husband's love ought to be for his wife as she actually

37

is—the particular woman whom God has given to him, with all her desires, joys, hopes, strengths, and weaknesses.

Jesus's love is sacrificial. How did Jesus show his love to the church? He "gave himself up for her." Paul is referring to Jesus's death on the cross, where he sacrificed his own life to save his bride. Jesus didn't merely pay lip service to loving us; he gave up his life for us. What an act of incredible self-giving love!

It is exactly this same kind of love that husbands are called to show for their wives. A Christian husband gives himself up for his wife—not by dying on the cross for her (she already has a Savior) but by putting her needs ahead of his own. A Christian husband will need to sacrifice his time, his ambitions, and his personal preferences in order to love his wife well.

This is a high calling, and only the power of the Holy Spirit can enable us to demonstrate even a faint shadow of Christ's love. But any Christian man who is not ready to engage seriously and prayerfully with this responsibility—any man who will insist on his rights and his desires over and against those of his wife—is simply not ready for marriage. And any Christian woman who is planning to marry a man who is not willing to love her in this way is planning to marry the wrong man.

Reflect: Husband-to-be, what do you think it will look like for you to love your fiancée as Christ loved the church? Are you ready to love sacrificially?

Reflect: Wife-to-be, what should you do when your future husband fails to live up to this standard (as he inevitably will)?

Act: Have a conversation with your fiancé about what sacrificial love might look like in your upcoming marriage. If you can, be specific.

DAY 11

Loving Your Wife Is Loving Yourself

In the same way husbands should love their wives as their own bodies. He who loves his wife loves himself. For no one ever hated his own flesh, but nourishes and cherishes it, just as Christ does the church, because we are members of his body. "Therefore a man shall leave his father and mother and hold fast to his wife, and the two shall become one flesh." (Eph. 5:28–31)

IN YESTERDAY'S READING, Paul made a connection between the love that Jesus showed for his church on the cross and the love that a husband should show for his wife. And, starting in verse 28 of the same chapter, Paul continues to explain what he means. After reiterating that "husbands should love their wives" in the "same way" that Jesus did, he adds another wrinkle—another image to help us understand what he is talking about. He talks about husbands loving their wives as their own bodies.

In verse 31, Paul quotes from the creation narrative (cf. Gen. 2:24) to show that when a man and a woman marry, they become bound together in a physical and spiritual union. We will come back to this on Day 15. For now, notice that everything Paul says in Ephesians 5:28–31 is based on the assumption that marriage creates a unity that's so powerful that it makes "one flesh" out of two people. Just as the church forms the body of her head, the Lord Jesus, in the same way a wife is intimately and vitally connected to her head—her husband (see Eph. 5:23).

Paul immediately seizes on the implications that this mysterious reality involves for husbands as they try to live out Christlike love. If a husband and wife are "one flesh," then it makes sense that husbands should think of their wives as extensions of themselves. When something good happens to a wife, it is as if it were happening to her husband too. When she experiences loss and sadness, then he does as well. When she flounders or struggles, so does he.

It's not hard to see the application that Paul makes from this principle—when a husband loves his wife, he is actually loving himself. One of the best ways for you to be happy as a husband is to care for and love your wife. When a husband serves, teaches, encourages, edifies, pours into, patiently listens to, and strengthens his wife, he is doing immense good for himself.

To be honest, I have never counseled a couple who both actually believed what Paul says here. It is easy for selfishness, distrust, and resentment to creep into a marriage and undermine a couple's sense of their unity. (They don't have the power to undo that unity through their neglect or anger, but they can make it hard for them to feel it.) And when that happens, husbands may imagine that they need to pursue their own joy—apart from or at the expense of their wives. In those moments, caring for your wife seems like the thing that is least likely to make you happy and well. In those moments, we believe and act on the truth—even if we don't "feel it."

Reflect: Husband-to-be, how do you need to grow in the area of loving and caring for your fiancée? If you are not sure, ask a mature Christian what it looks like for him to love his wife.

Reflect: How do you "nourish and cherish" your own body? How might you treat your spouse with similar care?

Act: Identify one thing that you might do differently, given that you and your spouse will be "one flesh."

DAY 12

God-Given Help

*Then the LORD God said, "It is not good that the man should be
alone; I will make him a helper fit for him." (Gen. 2:18)*

IF YOU HAVE read through the beginning of the book of Genesis, you may have noticed that a rhythm builds up over the course of creation. Multiple times across the third, fourth, fifth, and sixth days, God looks out over what he has made and sees that it is good—even "very good," in the case of the sixth day (see Gen. 1:31).

As a result, it comes as a shock when the narrative hits a snag in Genesis 2:18. After creating Adam and charging him to work and keep the garden of Eden, God declares that something about his creation is "not good." This doesn't mean God has made something substandard or unpleasant, but rather that something (or someone) is missing. Adam has been created well, but he was never designed to carry out his God-given mission alone. God's work of creation is not complete until he has made a woman—a wife—someone who can help Adam carry out God's design.

And so we are introduced to the first marriage, as well as to the role of the wife in the institution of marriage. Adam was created to rule over creation for God's glory—to tend the garden and fill the earth with more people (see Gen. 1:28). But he was not created with the ability to accomplish those tasks on his own. He needed a helper—someone who was like him (and thus the animals would not suffice—see Gen. 2:20) and yet different (and thus God did not create another male—see Gen. 2:22).

Again we see that men and women are created equal in terms of their dignity and significance. Adam calls Eve "flesh of my flesh" (Gen. 2:23), meaning that she is fundamentally the same as he is.

Whatever he is, she is too. She is not merely an animal—is not less than Adam. Instead, she is in every way "fit for" or "corresponding to" him (see v. 18, including alternate translation); she is Adam's equal in body, soul, and mind. And although it may be hard for us to wrap our modern minds around the concept, this first husband and first wife are created equal to each other but given different roles by their Creator—Eve is meant to help Adam to accomplish his God-given mission.

Now, a lot of Christian books and teachers will give you a lot of rules about how a wife is supposed to help her husband (involving things such as laundry, cooking, and staying home with children). And there may be merit to those suggestions, in many contexts. But it is important to acknowledge that the Bible does not give us a lot of specifics about what it means here for Eve to help her husband. In some arenas (for example, with respect to being fruitful and multiplying), her role is obvious. But otherwise, a husband and wife are left to work out what this will look like in their marriage. If a husband loves his wife as Christ loves the church, and if the wife has a heart that desires to joyfully help her husband, many of the specifics will work themselves out.

Reflect: What do you think it means to be a helper? Does helping someone make you somehow less than they are?

Reflect: God is often called our "help" throughout Scripture (see, for example, Ps. 46:1). What implications might this have for the way in which we think about the role of a wife in marriage?

Act: Talk with your fiancé about what this "helping" might look like practically in your future marriage.

DAY 13

Called to Submit

Wives, submit to your own husbands, as to the Lord. For the husband is the head of the wife even as Christ is the head of the church, his body, and is himself its Savior. Now as the church submits to Christ, so also wives should submit in everything to their husbands. (Eph. 5:22–24)

IN EPHESIANS 5, Paul instructs husbands and wives to occupy different roles in marriage. As we have already seen from earlier in that chapter, husbands are called on to lead and to show sacrificial love to their wives. In verses 22–24, wives are called on to submit to their husbands as their heads.

The word *submission* calls up all kinds of negative images—a submissive person might seem like a doormat, a loser, a weakling . . . maybe even a victim. But in reality, to be submissive simply means to be in proper relationship to an established authority. Consider three different types of people who live out a healthy picture of submission: a citizen follows the laws of the land, a solider executes the instructions of his commanding officer, and an athlete runs the play that her coach has called. In each case, the person's God-given role is to follow God-given authority. Submission, therefore, has nothing to do with being mistreated; it is simply a matter of acknowledging the authority of another person who is in a particular role.

In his wisdom, God has determined that within a marriage relationship the husband is meant to be the head of his wife. The wife is meant to follow the leadership of her husband in all the aspects of their life together—"in everything" (v. 24). There might be a lot of legitimate ways that we could add nuance to that statement—a wife shouldn't follow her husband into crime, abuse, or anything that is clearly contrary to God's will—but none of those unusual situations take away from the thrust of Paul's teaching that a wife is normally meant to submit to her husband.

What does that submission look like? Frankly, there is a lot of really poor teaching out there masquerading as biblical counsel on this question. The Bible does not give us a list of behaviors that constitute godly submission. We cannot say that a submissive wife always spends her days doing certain things and not others. Submission has little to do with which person chooses the restaurant or movie that you'll be enjoying that evening, who handles the family finances, or who drives the car.

Instead, the God-given role of a wife is to respond positively, even joyfully, to the leadership that her husband provides. Submission requires a wife to prayerfully support, encourage, and advise her husband as he directs the family under God's authority. A wife executes her role well when she acts as an indispensable key to her husband's success as the spiritual leader in the home.

Inevitably, a husband will make decisions with which his wife disagrees, and in those situations she should respectfully make her thoughts known. But she should never undermine him, belittle him, or secretly enjoy thoughts of his failure. A wife should work for the success and effectiveness of her husband (which, since they are one flesh, only helps her!).

Reflect: Why is it hard to be under authority? Think back over your life—which leaders have been the easiest for you to follow? Which have been the most difficult?

Act: Talk with your fiancé about what leadership and submission might look like in your marriage. Pray together that God might help you to live out your callings well.

DAY 14

A Beautiful Interplay

This is how the holy women who hoped in God used to adorn
themselves, by submitting to their own husbands, as Sarah obeyed
Abraham, calling him lord. And you are her children, if you do good
and do not fear anything that is frightening. Likewise, husbands,
live with your wives in an understanding way. (1 Peter 3:5–7)

IN TODAY'S PASSAGE, we focus on the way that Peter helps
wives and husbands to live out their calling in light of their roles.
What we find is that *submission* and *understanding* are key to a bib-
lically sound and successful marriage.

By its very nature, submission requires trust. Whether you
are an athlete executing the play that your coach has called or an
employee following your supervisor's instructions, being under
someone's authority requires you to trust that person's judgment
and leadership. And that trust makes you vulnerable—if your
coach calls a terrible play, you as the athlete will suffer the consequences on the field. If your supervisor gives bad directions, you
as the employee might lose a client's business.

This dynamic is present in marriage as well—and the stakes
are much higher. To follow a husband's lead can be frightening
(see 1 Peter 3:6); after all, he is just as fallible and sinful as the wife
is! But Peter calls wives not to give in to the fear that might make
them want to take over for their husbands. Instead he reminds
them that Sarai submitted to Abram even when he was being a
pretty lousy husband (cf. Gen. 12:11–16).

Instead of giving in to fear and trying to wrest control away
from their husbands, Sarai and the other "holy women" of the
Bible "hoped in God" (v. 5) and put their ultimate trust in the
leadership of their heavenly Father. They could submit to fallible

male leadership because they knew that God's care for them was infallible. Peter calls wives today to be like those admirable women—to do good and submit to their husbands, even when doing so is frightening.

In verse 7 he turns his attention to husbands. How should they live with their wives, with the knowledge that it can be scary to submit to another person? They should live in "an understanding way." A husband should seek to draw his wife out—to learn her thoughts and desires, her fears and hopes—and then to live with her in a way that shows respect and care for her. This requires the husband to treat his wife gently and considerately, for she is like fine china—precious and (comparatively) delicate. In this way, a husband shows his wife special honor.

You can see why it is so important for couples to take seriously the Lord's plan for husbands and wives. When wives strive for control or husbands refuse to sacrifice, marriage is painful and difficult. But when couples follow the divine design, marriage is a beautiful interplay of trust, care, love, and mutuality that glorifies God and brings them great joy.

Reflect: Husband-to-be, what can you do to better understand your future wife? Are there ways in which you can care for her with gentleness?

Reflect: Wife-to-be, do you find anything about submission to be frightening? How does the Lord's faithfulness give you strength?

Act: Create a plan for how you will handle a situation involving a serious disagreement about an important matter. How can the wife express her concerns well? Can you agree that you will be open to outside counsel if one or both of you find it necessary?

AN INTIMATE
RELATIONSHIP

DAY 15

A New Priority

*Then the man said, "This at last is bone of my bones and flesh of my
flesh. . . ." Therefore a man shall leave his father and his mother and
hold fast to his wife, and they shall become one flesh. And the man and
his wife were both naked and were not ashamed. (Gen. 2:23–25)*

WE SEE IN Genesis 2:21–22 that God used one of the man's
ribs to fashion the woman—a fitting companion for him. Adam
responded by breaking out into verse. You can well understand
his joy—after futilely searching through all the animal kingdom,
he realized, "Here (at last!) is someone like me! This woman's
bones are the same as mine; her flesh is just like mine!"

The author of Genesis then draws out two important truths
about marriage in verses 24 and 25.

*The fact that Eve was created from Adam explains why marriage
is a prioritized relationship.* Initially, the most important people
in a human being's life are his or her parents. Our mothers and
fathers are meant to be a source of care, provision, identity, and
nurture for us in the most formative years of our lives. Children
are meant to honor their parents (see Ex. 20:12) and show loyalty
to their family of origin.

But in Genesis 2, we learn that "a man shall leave his father and
his mother and hold fast to his wife." Although the text of Genesis
2 speaks specifically of a man leaving his father and mother, we
are safe to apply this principle to women as well (in fact, it would
be difficult to understand how it could work otherwise). Both
husbands and wives must leave their parents—physically (which
normally means moving out and finding your own place) and
emotionally (which means that Mom and Dad are no longer the
people you turn to first for help, support, and encouragement).

In their place, a married couple cling to each other. They are each other's top priority, humanly speaking. Early on in a marriage, this is often a point of contention. Many parents are used to having a prominent voice in their kids' lives, and they may not understand that they can no longer have that kind of influence once a son or daughter is married. When there is conflict in your new marriage, it can be tempting for you to turn to your parents for consolation and vindication (after all, your parents are probably going to be on "your side"). And while there may be wisdom in getting input from your parents from time to time, it's important for you to establish clearly that the best of your loyalty and affection belongs to your spouse. You must cling to each other and make it clear that other good things (your parents, children, and careers) will have to be less important.

Adam and Eve show that marriage is a transparent relationship. Because Adam and Eve were one flesh, they were both naked and unashamed. They had nothing to hide from each other (and it helped that they were also sinless at this point in the narrative!) and no sense that they ought to be ashamed of anything. Even after our fall into sin, marriage is a relationship in which a man and a woman can be open and known. There ought to be no secrets, no hiding, and no shame. Ideally, your spouse would know you the way that you know yourself.

Reflect: God designed marriage to give us some sense of what his love is like. In light of that truth, what does Genesis 2:24 teach us about God's love for us?

Act: Talk with your fiancé about your relationship with your parents. Are they likely to respect the priority of your new marriage?

DAY 16

'Til Death Do Us Part

"'God made them male and female.' 'Therefore a man shall leave his father and mother and hold fast to his wife, and the two shall become one flesh.' So they are no longer two but one flesh. What therefore God has joined together, let not man separate." (Mark 10:6–9)

THERE IS SOME debate about the exact statistics, but there can be no doubt that Christians get divorced at a shocking rate. There are divorced men and women in the church that I pastor, and several of the marriages that I have officiated have ended in divorce. I am currently working with several couples who may very well wind up ending their marriages as well.

My friend, it should not be so. In Mark 10, Jesus reminds us that God designed marriage to create a deep physical and spiritual unity between a husband and wife. When the Lord has "joined together" a man and a woman, no human being should separate them. The marriage commitment you are planning to make is meant to last until death finally separates you (see Rom. 7:2). There is no test drive, no warranty, no return policy. If you are not ready to sign up for that kind of commitment, then you are not ready to get married.

Marriage is meant to display God's character. When God makes a covenant with his people, he is relentlessly faithful to it. He always does everything that he says he will do. When his people sin against him, he continues to love them. When they are unfaithful to him, he continues to show them mercy. As we saw in days 2 and 3, our sin is a kind of adultery. As such, God has had countless reasons to wash his hands of us, but his lovingkindness never fails. His faithfulness is our only hope for eternal life. If our salvation depended on our faithfulness to God, we would all be lost. But we can praise God that his love never fails.

In the same way, when a couple enters into a marriage covenant, they are meant to be unfailingly faithful to each other. As hard as it might be to imagine right now, there may be times in the future when you would prefer not to be married to each other. I hope that it is not the case, but it is possible that your marriage will be more difficult and unpleasant than you might imagine. If for some reason you are not ready to make a commitment to stay together even if that happens, then you are not ready to get married.

I believe that there are some circumstances (such as unrepentant unfaithfulness, violence, and abandonment) that make divorce a proper course of action. In such cases, divorce is not a sin—rather, the behaviors that necessitate the divorce are the real issue. But most divorces do not arise from these kinds of extreme situations.

I sincerely hope your marriage will be a source of great joy throughout your entire life. But if your spouse isn't as wonderful as you hope that he or she will be, if marriage turns out to be difficult and wearying, know that God is giving you an opportunity to reflect his character more clearly. You can be sure that your faithfulness to your spouse will never outshine the Lord's faithfulness to you.

Reflect: Are you prepared to give yourself to your fiancé for a lifetime, even if your marriage doesn't go the way that you think it will?

Act: Talk with your fiancé about divorce. Make sure that you are on the same page about the nature of the commitment you are both entering into.

DAY 17

The Gift of Intimacy

How beautiful and pleasant you are, O loved one, with all your delights!
... Oh may your breasts be like clusters of the vine, and the scent of your
breath like apples, and your mouth like the best wine. (Song 7:6, 8–9)

WHEN IT COMES TO SEX, Christianity has gotten a bad rap.
Perhaps some of it has been well earned; the church at times
has taken an unhelpful stance toward sex. But it should not be
so. After all, sex was God's idea—there is even an entire book of
the Bible (Song of Songs) that is essentially a collection of erotic
poetry! Sex is a very good gift that God has given to us, and so we
would do well to seek to understand its role in a marriage.

When we look at the Bible's teaching on sex, we can identify
three main purposes for which God created it.

- *Reproduction.* This one isn't hard to understand. Sex is the
  means by which we fulfill our mandate to "multiply" (Gen.
  1:28).
- *Pleasure.* Sex is meant to be enjoyable. God could have
  designed a far less enjoyable way for humans to reproduce, so
  it seems significant that he chose to make sex so wonderfully
  pleasurable. Married couples are free to enjoy this good gift
  simply for the pleasure of it, as they give gratitude to God for
  his kindness.
- *Intimacy.* Sex is not a purely physical act. As a man and a woman
  connect their bodies, they form an emotional and spiritual
  bond as well. (This unity that comes through intimacy is what
  Paul has in view when he instructs us in 1 Corinthians 6 to
  refrain from sexual immorality. Paul wants us to save intimacy
  for marriage!)

There is much more to marriage than sex. If a husband or wife is for some reason unable to regularly have sex, that doesn't mean that their marriage is doomed. But normally sex will serve as both a thermostat and a thermometer for your relationship. It's like a thermostat in that it can "heat things up"—can be used to build, maintain, and even restore waning intimacy in a marriage. It's also a thermometer in that it can indicate the "temperature" of a relationship—the frequency and quality of sexual intimacy can be a helpful data point for how a marriage is going.

As you might well imagine, a couple's sexual relationship will look different throughout the years. Over time you will get to know each other's bodies and preferences much better. But over the years (Lord willing!), pregnancies, young children and teenagers in the home, and the changes that take place in your bodies will affect what happens in the bedroom.

It is really important for you and your spouse to be committed to regular, honest communication on this topic. Men and women have different (though compatible) experiences of sexual desire and pleasure. It is unlikely that you will understand what your spouse finds pleasurable and attractive unless you ask them and listen.

Reflect: Take a moment to think about your own expectations regarding sex in your marriage. Are there any expectations or desires that you might need to change in order to glorify God and serve your partner in this area?

Act: In order to avoid temptation, you will need to be careful about how and when you talk about sex with your fiancé before the wedding. Find a godly married person of your same gender and ask them her what they wish they had known about sex when they first got married.

DAY 18

The Gift of Exclusivity

Let marriage be held in honor among all, and let the
marriage bed be undefiled, for God will judge the
sexually immoral and adulterous. (Heb. 13:4)

FOR DECADES, some people have been working diligently to establish the ordinariness of sex in our wider world. In many places, the notion that sex is special, meaningful, or significant lies somewhere between being old-fashioned and ludicrous. Many are highly invested in viewing sex as a purely physical interaction that has no deeper purpose. As long as everyone consents to it, there is no greater moral meaning to be found from it. Your choices regarding sex are no more significant than your choice of hairstyle or what you like to eat for breakfast.

But God doesn't share our world's low opinion of his handiwork. The one who created sex is the one who determines its meaning. We are reminded in Hebrews 13 (and in many other places in Scripture; see Col. 3:5–6 for one example) that God will pass judgment on those who distort his gift and use it for their own purposes. We are not free to use our sexuality in just any way that we would like. The train of our sexuality is meant to run on the tracks of a faithful, exclusive marriage relationship.

If you are not yet married, you should not be engaging in any sexual behavior with your fiancé (or with anyone else, for that matter). This is important, because sexual temptation often becomes more intense the closer you get to your wedding day. You might think, "What's the big deal? After all, we are going to get married!" But there are at least two really good reasons for you to wait until after your wedding.

- *God says not to.* He's going to judge the sexually immoral. A few moments of pleasure are not worth incurring God's discipline.
- *It is a terrible foundation for your upcoming life together.* Imagine how damaging it will be for both of you to know beyond a shadow of a doubt that if your spouse is sufficiently tempted sexually, they are willing to do things that they know are wrong.

Sexual immorality—and particularly adultery—is a grievous sin that ruins people's lives. It might seem inconceivable to you now that you would ever cheat on your spouse, but I have lost track of the number of Christian marriages that have been destroyed by a spouse's infidelity. Marriage can be difficult at times, and there may well be people who will give you the things that you feel you are not getting from your spouse. Don't go near such temptation! Keep yourself far from anyone to whom you might be attracted and from people who might wrongly be attracted to you.

Marriage was created for a purpose and with a meaning. It is a picture of Christ's love for his bride, the church. We never have to wonder whether Jesus will be faithful in his love for us. And so we must always be faithful to our spouses.

Reflect: Proverbs 5 presents a haunting picture of the devastation that is wrought by adultery. Three thousand years later, it still feels very applicable. Read that chapter prayerfully and consider how you personally might experience the temptation to be unfaithful to your spouse.

Act: Talk with your fiancé about what "policies" you might want to institute regarding your interactions with potential sources of temptation. For example: I won't ride in a car alone with another woman.

A HOLY RELATIONSHIP

DAY 19

God's Will for Your Life

As obedient children, do not be conformed to the passions
of your former ignorance, but as he who called you is holy,
you also be holy in all your conduct, since it is written, "You
shall be holy, for I am holy." (1 Peter 1:14–16)

WHY ARE YOU getting married? What do you hope to accomplish together with your spouse? When you picture married life, what do you envision?

There are good answers to these questions, of course. Maybe you picture a lifetime of raising children, building a home, sharing experiences, and going on vacations together. All these things are good, and I hope that God blesses you with them. But, as much as I hate to say it, none of those things are guaranteed.

The great theologian B. B. Warfield married Annie Kinkead in 1876. The young couple set off for Europe shortly thereafter, until one day they were caught in a thunderstorm while walking in the Harz Mountains. Annie was never the same again. She suffered the rest of her life with a "nervous disorder" and was unable to have children. As a result, Warfield never spent more than a couple of consecutive hours away from their home, thereby refusing the increased fame and money that could have been his had he traveled and given lectures.

That is obviously an extreme example, but it illustrates an inescapable reality: no one but God knows what our future will hold. Married couples can plan and dream, but God will ordain their steps.

In light of all that we cannot know about the future, it is helpful for us to be clear about the things we *do* know that God has said he will accomplish in our lives. And while he does not promise that our lives will always be marked by ease, pleasure, and comfort, he does promise to help us to grow in holiness.

That is what Peter is pointing to in today's passage. All God's children, whether married or not, are called to look like their Father in heaven. He is holy, and so we are to be holy as well. That is God's clear and unambiguous stated will for our lives (see 1 Thess. 4:3).

Can you see the implications that this has for marriage? If God is concerned with our holiness, then he is going to orchestrate our lives (and our marriages!) to help us to grow to be more like him. But that may mean that we will have to walk through difficult and painful circumstances that we wouldn't have chosen for ourselves. Certainly that was the case for the Warfields.

Disappointment can be traced to our expectations. When your expectations are out of alignment with reality, you become set up for disappointment. If you go into marriage with your heart set on fun, ease, and pleasure, you may find yourself disappointed when God's agenda turns out to be different from yours. Many of the common problems that surface in marriage can be traced back to this basic idea—couples struggle when their marriages aren't fulfilling their expectations. In the end, we don't put our hope in our circumstances. Instead, we trust that our loving heavenly Father is in control of everything that comes our way.

Reflect: Think about your expectations for your marriage. How will you react if things don't work out the way that you want?

Act: Find a Christian couple whose marriage you respect. Ask them about unexpected challenges they have faced and how those challenges have helped them to grow in holiness.

DAY 20

Fruit Grows in the
Soil of Relationships

Now the works of the flesh are evident: sexual immorality, impurity,
sensuality, idolatry, sorcery, enmity, strife, jealousy, fits of anger, rivalries,
dissensions, divisions, envy, drunkenness, orgies, and things like these.
... But the fruit of the Spirit is love, joy, peace, patience, kindness,
goodness, faithfulness, gentleness, self-control. (Gal. 5:19–23)

IN JUST TWO SENTENCES, Paul paints a vivid picture of
two radically different ways of life. One is characterized by the
"works of the flesh"—conflict, hatred, and sinful indulgence. The
other is lived out under the influence of God's Holy Spirit, who
brings forth a grocery store's worth of good "fruit" in the lives of
his people.

Christians will doubtlessly read the first list with a mixture
of revulsion and regret. Our stomachs turn when we think about
how terrible it would be to be trapped in a life marked by fits of
anger and envy and impurity, and we also hate the ways that these
things still encroach on us and tempt us daily. Conversely, we read
about the fruit of the Spirit with a mixture of gratitude and longing—gratitude that we can see some of these things growing on
the formerly barren branches of our lives, and longing because
we have tasted how good it is to live under the Spirit's rule and we
want so much more of it.

Have you ever noticed how many of the works of the flesh
and the fruits of the Spirit require a relationship in order to exist?
Things like rivalries, divisions, and enmity are sins of relationship. You have to have someone else to hate and envy; if you had
somehow grown up alone on a deserted island, you probably
would not be tempted to be jealous. It is only when we come into

contact with others who have what we want that our flesh produces the work of envy.

In the same way, so many of the good qualities that the Spirit produces in us seem to imply a relationship. The fruit of love requires an object—a beloved. Patience grows and is exercised in the context of an interaction with someone who is inconveniencing me or failing to meet my expectations. I need someone to whom I can be kind and faithful.

The holiness that God wants for us (remember yesterday?) looks like these fruits of the Spirit. God the Holy Spirit makes us look like himself—makes us patient and loving and joyful. And that holiness happens in the context of relationships with other people. That is much of the glory of belonging to a local church—God brings us into a body with other people so that we can help one another to grow more like him.

Can you see what that means for your marriage? The intimacy of the relationship means that your future spouse is the one person who is most likely to provoke and draw out the works of your flesh. A God-honoring marriage will look a lot like a husband and wife growing in those fruits of the Spirit through the ways that they interact with each other.

Reflect: Which of the works of the flesh are most likely to characterize your relationship with your fiancé? Which of the fruit of the Spirit are you most lacking?

Act: If you find yourself becoming angry or impatient with your fiancé, discipline yourself to look at yourself first. Most of the time, a problem that you are experiencing with another person is located not primarily within the other person but within your heart. Pray that the Holy Spirit would help you to grow in love, peace, patience, and kindness.

DAY 21

Without Spot or Wrinkle

Husbands, love your wives, as Christ loved the church and gave himself up for her, that he might sanctify her, having cleansed her by the washing of water with the word, so that he might present the church to himself in splendor, without spot or wrinkle or any such thing, that she might be holy and without blemish. (Eph. 5:25–27)

AS WE HAVE SEEN, Ephesians 5 is like a rich mine—it is full of gold for married couples. As we turn yet again to this passage, we get to meditate even more on what Jesus has done for his people.

In verse 26, Paul reminds us of the great purpose behind Christ's lovingly sacrificing himself. Christ gave himself for his church so "that he might sanctify her." In this context, to "sanctify" someone or something means to make it holy for the Lord's service. Jesus does this for his people by cleansing them "by the washing of water with the word." It is not 100 percent clear what Paul means by this phrase—some scholars think that this is a reference to the symbolism of baptism; others see here a reference to where the Lord speaks of washing Israel and preparing her to be his bride (see Ezek. 16:1–14). But in any event, what is clear is that Jesus's sacrificial death has the effect of cleansing his people. He presents her as a bride "in splendor"—like a garment that is fresh from the cleaners without a spot or wrinkle. She is made spiritually "holy and without blemish."

Yet again, we have to be astounded that this is the model of love that husbands are called to emulate. A husband's love for his wife is not expressed primarily through bringing her flowers or taking her out on romantic dates (though those things are good, and husbands should do them!). Rather, the love and leadership of a Christian husband plays itself out in his selflessly helping his wife to grow in holiness.

Once embraced, this model of love will inform every area of a couple's relationship. A husband serves his wife by paying careful attention to his own spiritual growth. After all, you cannot lead your wife into anything that you don't have yourself. If you are not growing in Christ, it will be hard for you to help someone else grow. Meanwhile, a wife can make it easier for her husband to lead in this way by being open and responding positively when he tries to point out areas in her life that are in need of growth.

A main way that we grow in holiness is through the Word of God (did you notice that at the end of verse 26?). Take time to read God's Word together and on your own. A husband may put this passage into action by taking small children for a while so that his wife can read the Bible and pray. Good leadership also involves taking the initiative to find and join a faithful church and to get connected with other believers there so that a couple can hear God's Word together on Sunday mornings and live it out during the week in a community.

Reflect: Jesus died in order to make us holy. We are perfectly righteous in God's sight now, even though we still sin. We are meant to help one another (by the power of the Spirit) to grow to look more like Jesus. Why do you think God set it up that way? What do we learn, and gain, from this process?

Act: Talk together about what it might look like for you and your fiancé to grow in holiness once you are married. What things can you do together? What habits can you form?

DAY 22

The Value of Input

The ear that listens to life-giving reproof will dwell among the wise. Whoever ignores instruction despises himself, but he who listens to reproof gains intelligence. (Prov. 15:31–32)

WE HAVE BEEN thinking about the truth of how God has designed the institution of marriage in part to help his people to grow in holiness. Today we consider a very practical way in which a husband and wife can help each other to grow: through criticism.

You might be feeling tempted to skip over this reading. After all, no one likes to be criticized. But there are two realities that make it important for you to have people in your life who are willing to point out your faults, mistakes, and unhelpful ways of thinking.

We are all sinners. Unless you are perfect (and I am working with the Bible's assessment that you are not), you are going to do things that are wrong. You will react badly to the sin of others. Your ways of thinking about the world won't always match up with reality as God describes it. Some of these things have been taught to you in your family of origin; others you have developed on your own.

The nature of sin is such that it blinds us to its presence. Even though we are made new in Christ, indwelling sin continues to plague us (see Rom. 7). Our hearts deceive us (see Jer. 17:9), and we are unable to see the truth about ourselves clearly. We tend to excuse our failings and to think of ourselves much more highly than we ought.

Marriage is a wonderful gift that God has given to help us to grow in grace and holiness. Because your spouse lives with you and is the person who is most impacted by your sin, they will be able to see some things about you that you would probably never recognize on your own. Things like pride, irritability, and selfishness might be hard for us to recognize in ourselves. But you can be sure that your spouse will see them! One of the great benefits of marriage is that you have someone around who loves you, who is committed to your holiness, and who sees some aspects of your life to which you are blind. If the wounds that are given by a friend are faithful (see Prov. 27:6), how much more so are those that are given by a loving spouse!

There are, however, obstacles to the development of this healthy dynamic in a marriage. When pride is left unchecked, it is easy for a person to see loving correction as nagging or insulting. Insecurity can interpret even the gentlest rebuke as a serious threat. I have seen marriages spiral out of control because one or both members could not bear to be corrected. For example, when a wife raises a concern but her husband will not take it seriously, it is easy for her to develop bitterness and irritability toward him. She might then be tempted to nag in order to be heard. That tempts him to tune her out and ignore her feelings. Once you are in a cycle like this (usually without realizing it at first), it is really hard for you to break out.

God wants you to be holy, and—as he does with so many things—he often uses other people to accomplish this purpose. Your spouse is a gift to you to help you see problems that you would not otherwise know about.

Reflect: Do you handle criticism well? Have you ever thought about the way that the Bible encourages us not just to accept correction but to actually seek it out?

Act: Ask your fiancé if there are any ways in which you need to grow or change that they haven't felt free to talk with you about. What does the dynamic that today's reading discussed look like in your relationship?

DAY 23

A Marriage in Community

*Older men are to be sober-minded, dignified, self-controlled, sound
in faith, in love, and in steadfastness. Older women likewise are
to be reverent in behavior, not slanderers or slaves to much wine.
They are to teach what is good, and so train the young women
. . . that the word of God may not be reviled. (Titus 2:2–5)*

ONE OF THE most important things that you can do for your
marriage is to become a member of a healthy, gospel-preaching
church. After all, we have seen that Jesus's love is given not to
humanity in general or to a series of disconnected individuals but
rather to his church (see Eph. 5:25).

Paul's instructions to Titus in today's passage show us that
the church is the context in which individual Christians are to
be shaped, formed, and brought into maturity. If that is the case
for Christian individuals, how much more is it so for Christian
couples? You will need to be part of a church in order to have the
God-honoring marriage that you ought to have.

Let me suggest six ways in which being part of a healthy
church can help you to strengthen your marriage.

Peer friendship. Over the years, my wife and I have been greatly
helped by other couples who are at our same stage of life. We have
been able to share with them the joys and challenges of being
newlyweds, of having young children and then teenagers, and so
on. The best place to find people like this is in a healthy church.

Service. Church membership calls us outside ourselves and
gives us a context for serving others. It is good for you to be
reminded that you two are not the most important people in the
world. Couples who serve the body of Christ will find it more
natural to serve each other in marriage.

Leaders. Jesus has given his people Spirit-empowered leaders for the good of their souls (see Eph. 4:11–12; Heb. 13:17). Being a member of a church puts you under the spiritual care of such leaders; hearing them teach God's Word week in and week out will strengthen you—both personally and as a couple.

Accountability. When you join a church, you are asking to be held accountable for your Christian behavior and commitments (see 1 Cor. 5:1–2). The fellowship of the church is one of God's ways of protecting his people from the deceitfulness of sin (see Heb. 3:12–13).

Connection. You and your spouse might be able to manage well enough on your own, as long as everything goes well. But if something goes wrong—sickness, sadness, sin—you may find that it is too late to get make connections and get the help of a local church. Be a committed part of a church now so that you have the help when you need it.

Exposure to older generations. It is good for you to have relationships with Christians who have walked further down the path of life than you have. Paul tells Titus to make sure that older people in the church are caring for the younger people and teaching them how to follow Jesus. As younger people come into contact with the life of the church, they will be able to observe, and be instructed by, godly older men and women.

Reflect: Evaluate your current church situation—is your church focused on the gospel? Is your level of involvement going to be helpful in your upcoming marriage?

Act: Talk to a pastor about your upcoming marriage. Ask about how you can be involved in the church in a way that will serve others well and strengthen your marriage.

DAY 24

A Marriage of Perfectly Righteous People

If we say we have no sin, we deceive ourselves, and the truth is not in us. If we confess our sins, he is faithful and just to forgive us our sins and to cleanse us from all unrighteousness. (I John 1:8–9)

ON DAY 22, we considered the importance of being open to criticism and discussed why so many find that openness difficult—our hearts are often proud, and we long to be thought of as better than we really are. What can we do to cultivate humility so that we can better embrace correction? How does the gospel help us to take criticism and correction well? Let me suggest two things.[1]

The gospel makes us aware of our failures. The message of Christ crucified is a message of our great need for salvation. On our own, we were enemies of God (see Rom. 5:10) and were imprisoned by our lusts and sinful desires (see 1 Peter 1:14). In fact, we were so lost and depraved that the only way we could be saved was for the Son of God to bear the terrible wrath of God in our place.

When we look at Jesus's suffering on the cross, we see what our sin deserves. The cross is God's criticism of us. It is his statement of what we deserve. If that is the case, then we should be open to whatever criticism and correction our spouses offer us. If they observe that we have patterns of selfishness or a lack of love, our pride tempts us to become angry and begin an argument. But when we look at the cross, we have to admit that actually, far

---

1. See Alfred J. Poirier, "The Cross and Criticism," *The Journal of Biblical Counseling* 17, no. 3 (Spring 1999): 17. The ideas in this day's reading come largely from my reflections on this excellent article; it is no exaggeration to say that God used it to save my marriage.

worse is true of us than what our spouses say. Any sin that they see in us is a tiny fraction of the whole reality.

The gospel shows us that we are completely justified by the finished work of Christ. When someone points out our faults, we often want to justify ourselves. We long to be thought of as blameless. We might be tempted to argue and attack in order to feel vindicated. But in Jesus, we have already been given everything that we are tempted to fight for. Because we are in Christ, we have been utterly cleansed from all our guilt. Every one of our sins was laid upon him at the cross, and we bear them no more.

Can you see how this truth can impact your marriage? If both of you think too highly of yourselves, if you have not really wrestled with what the Bible says about your sin, then you will not be open when your spouse points out areas of your life that are in need of correction. And if you have not really internalized what it means that, despite your sin, you are 100 percent righteous in Christ, then you will always be forced to justify yourself when you are criticized. But two people who really grasp the message of the cross will be quick to acknowledge their faults when they are pointed out ("After all, I know that worse is true about me!") and will not feel as if their world is collapsing when attention is brought to their shortcomings ("After all, I know that God sees me as perfect in Christ!").

Reflect: How do you normally respond to criticism? How does reflecting on the gospel message help you to embrace correction?

Act: Talk with your fiancé about the ways that you both give and receive correction. What would make it easier for your fiancé to receive the correction that you offer?

LIFE TOGETHER

DAY 25

The Power of Words

*The L*ORD *passed before him and proclaimed, "The L*ORD*, the*
L*ORD*, a God merciful and gracious, slow to anger, and abounding*
in steadfast love and faithfulness. . . ." And Moses quickly bowed
his head toward the earth and worshiped. (Ex. 34:6, 8)

YOU MIGHT BE wondering whether today's reading belongs in
a book for engaged couples. After all, what does Exodus 34 have
to do with marriage? Well, in a sense, not much. But it does tell us
a lot about the God who designed marriage, and so it has plenty
for us to learn.

What we want to look at today is not so much what God
reveals about himself but rather *how* he reveals himself. If you
remember the context, Moses made a request to see God's glory
(see Ex. 33:18), but instead of *showing* himself to Moses God
explained himself to Moses. He told Moses what he was like.
He could have used any number of means to communicate to
Moses what his character and nature are like—he could have
painted a picture, carved a sculpture, taken a photograph, made
a diorama. But God chose to speak—to reveal himself in articu-
lated words.

And, in fact, it had always been that way. The first thing that
we see God doing in the Bible is speaking—creating the world by
pronouncing it into existence. Then, after he made Adam and Eve,
they needed him to speak to them in order to explain the world
and why they were there and what they were supposed to do (see
Gen. 1:28). When God wanted Abraham or Isaac or Jacob to do
something or know something, he spoke to them (see, for example, Gen. 46:2–4).

What does all this have to do with marriage? Everything!

Our Creator has woven the power of the spoken word deep into the fabric of our world. We cannot speak things into existence like he can, but according to the Bible our words have the power to

- destroy the people who are closest to us (see Prov. 11:9)
- stir up anger or calm it down (see Prov. 15:1)
- bring life and health to a relationship or crush someone's spirit (see Prov. 15:4)
- act as life-giving water for someone's soul (see Prov. 18:4)
- damage someone like a weapon of war (see Prov. 25:18)
- reveal things that are hiding in our hearts (see Luke 6:45)

We could go on and on heaping up examples. And over the next few days we will fill in some details. But for today, we have just one important truth to meditate upon: much of the trajectory and temperature of your marriage will be set by the words that you speak to each other. One of the most important ways in which your marriage will reflect the character of our speaking God is through your words.

Reflect: Think about the power that words have had in your life. If you think of yourself as smart or good-looking or as a good friend, it's likely because someone said that you were at some point in your life. If you have a negative opinion of yourself, there's a pretty good chance that those feelings have roots in words that were spoken to you.

Act: Keep a careful watch on the words that you speak to your fiancé today. What do you notice about the way that you speak? What impact do your words (in terms of both what you say and how you say it) have on the other person?

DAY 26

Speech That Builds Up

*Gracious words are like a honeycomb, sweetness to the
soul and health to the body. (Prov. 16:24)*

*Let no corrupting talk come out of your mouths, but only
such as is good for building up, as fits the occasion, that
it may give grace to those who hear. (Eph. 4:29)*

IN YESTERDAY'S READING, we thought about the power
of the words that we use—both for good and for ill. Today, let's
think about how gracious and wise words can help to build a
healthy marriage.

Proverbs 16 gives us a vivid image when it tells us that gracious
words are like a honeycomb. When someone speaks graciously—
with words that are kind, encouraging, focused on the good, and
quick to forgive—the effect is the emotional equivalent of gulping
down a big spoonful of honey. Gracious words make people feel
better deep down in their souls and even can bring health to their
bodies.

In Ephesians 4, the apostle Paul contrasts "corrupting talk"—
speech that corrodes and weakens—with words that are "good
for building up." Edifying words "[fit] the occasion"—sometimes
your words need to be bold; sometimes they need to be gentle—
and they can communicate grace to those who hear them.

Marriage is supposed to be the image of God's love for his
people. The way that a husband sacrificially loves his wife and
that a wife joyfully helps and follows her husband is a lived-out
picture of the grace of God. And there are few arenas in which
a married couple will live out the gospel together that are more
important than the words that they speak to each other.

Husbands are called to live out the gospel by living with their wives in an understanding way. An understanding husband speaks gracious, patient, sympathetic words. He will ask good questions to draw out his wife so that he can know her better—will make it clear to her that she does not have to pretend to be something she is not in order to earn his love.

Wives are told to live out the gospel by showing respect to their husbands. A respectful wife will speak encouraging, positive, honoring words. When she needs to correct or disagree with her husband (and there are times when love means telling someone something that they do not want to hear!), she will speak in a way that still communicates respect. She will not make her husband perform to a certain level before she will speak to him with grace.

Words are important, because they reveal the thoughts and attitudes that are hidden deep down in our hearts (see Luke 6:45). And because our speech springs up from the attitudes of our hearts, the only way for us to have marriages that are marked by a consistent pattern of gracious words over the long haul is for us to deeply internalize the truth of the gospel. The best way for you to grow in your capacity for speaking life-giving, honey-sweet gracious words is to meditate on God's forgiving, patient, unmerited, sacrificial love. When that love is massaged deep into your heart, it will spring out in the words that you speak to your spouse.

Reflect: Speak with your fiancé about the way that you talk to each other. How could you communicate grace to each other more effectively?

Act: Make a point to say something today that reflects to your fiancé the way that God has loved them in Christ.

DAY 27

The Easy Way to Destroy Everything

The tongue is a fire, a world of unrighteousness. The tongue is set among our members . . . setting on fire the entire course of life, and set on fire by hell. For every kind of beast . . . can be tamed and has been tamed by mankind, but no human being can tame the tongue. It is a restless evil, full of deadly poison. (James 3:6–8)

JAMES COMPARES THE tongue to a fire—and what an apt picture that is! When they are misused, both fire and the tongue can wreak incredible damage. A tiny spark can burn down an entire forest, and a careless word can wreck a marriage.

In light of what James says, it should come as no surprise that marital problems and communication problems often go together.

Speech may be irritable. Living with someone else can be annoying. They may not do things the way that you would do them or prioritize the same things that you do. Instead of confronting those issues in an honest and caring way, it is much easier to fall into a pattern of venting your frustration through little barbs and jabs. If you have ever been around a married couple who constantly bicker over unimportant things, then you have seen the way that irritable words tear down intimacy.

Speech may be critical. Marriage gives you a front-row seat to the faults and flaws of another human being. If you want to be critical of your spouse, you will probably find plenty of material to work with. But no one thrives and flourishes in an environment in which they are constantly being corrected and criticized. And so if the regular diet of your communication with your spouse consists of complaining or pointing out their flaws, don't be surprised when they don't want to spend much time with you.

Speech may be mocking. A lot of guys express their affection by making fun of one another. In my experience, wives do not enjoy being treated this way. It's a good policy in your marriage to commit to never mocking, belittling, or complaining about your spouse.

Speech may be angry. Probably my biggest regrets in life are related to things that I have said in anger. Rightly did the Lord Jesus equate anger with murder (see Matt. 5:21–22), because an angry person wants to destroy the object of their rage. Needless to say, angry words will destroy the intimacy that is meant to characterize a marriage.

In order to protect your marriage from the destructive power of the tongue, you will need to learn self-control. Rightly does James tell us that we should be quick to hear and slow to speak (see James 1:19). But in the end, he also reminds us that no human can tame his or her tongue merely through effort and discipline (see James 3:8). Our only hope is in the gospel of Jesus Christ as it is applied by the power of the Holy Spirit. We need hearts that are captured by the truth that, while we were still in our sins, God spoke words of love and forgiveness to us through his Son.

Reflect: Think about your fiancé's weaknesses and faults. How does God view those faults in light of the gospel? How can you speak to your spouse in a way that models the gospel's message of undeserved love and forgiveness?

Act: Pray Psalm 141:3 together with your fiancé.

DAY 28

Anger and Conflict

What causes quarrels and what causes fights among you?
Is it not this, that your passions are at war within you? You
desire and do not have, so you murder. You covet and cannot
obtain, so you fight and quarrel. (James 4:1–2)

"WHAT CAUSES OUR FIGHTS?" "Why are we fighting?"
Married couples often ask such questions when they come to me
for help. "Why are we experiencing so much friction?" "Why are
we bickering over seemingly unimportant things?"

In my experience, spouses normally come preloaded with
answers to these questions. "We fight because he won't listen to
me. He doesn't care." "We bicker because she is always criticizing
me. She is never happy." "We have conflict because he doesn't do
his share around the house. I have to be his mother." "We argue
because she doesn't want to have sex as often as I'd like." All those
things may well be true (in fact, they usually *are* true), and they
may in fact be the occasion of many fights. But James 4 tells us
that none of those things are the reason for the conflict that we
have. According to the Bible, we do not have conflict because
people sin against us. Rather, we have conflict because our "passions are at war" within us. When we want something and don't
get it, we are willing to become angry and fight. James calls this a
kind of "murder," riffing on Jesus's teaching in Matthew 5:21–22.
When we do not get what we want, we become angry. When we
are denied our deepest desires, we become willing to go to war.

If you understand this idea, it will have a massive impact on
your marriage. We are generally taught to think of anger as a force
that builds up inside us—as something that is disconnected from
our true selves. So we learn to deal with anger accordingly; we

bottle it up, blow off steam, or have a venting session. We learn to count to ten. We take a walk around the block. We punch a pillow until our rage is exhausted. But these things are merely ways of dealing with the symptoms of anger and of limiting the damage done by our anger.

The Bible says that our anger comes from our passionate commitment to get what we want. It's not necessarily that we love the wrong things (it is good to want your spouse to clean up after themselves or to listen to you or to have sex). The problem is that we love those good things *too much*—we love them more than we love God and obedience to his ways. We make idols out of our desires. And so when someone (such as our spouse) gets in the way of our getting our hearts' desire, we become angry. When they fail to serve our idols, we gear up for battle. If they stand in the way of what we want, we will go to war.

We experience conflict because our hearts have been captured by inordinate desires. It's not a pretty picture, but it is accurate. It may not be the happiest diagnosis, but it is the first step toward finding the cure.

Reflect: Think back on the last time you were angry (whether it was explosive and loud or cold and icy). Can you identify what it was that you wanted so badly in that situation? Can you see how you made it into an idol?

Act: Discipline yourself to speak about your anger correctly. Don't say "You make me angry when . . ."; but rather be ruthlessly honest about what it is that you want in the situation. Sometimes dragging your desires out into the light helps you to see how ugly they are.

Repentance Is the Way Forward

But he gives more grace. Therefore it says, "God opposes the proud but gives grace to the humble." Submit yourselves therefore to God. . . . Be wretched and mourn and weep. . . . Humble yourselves before the Lord, and he will exalt you. (James 4:6–7, 9–10)

I ONCE MET with a man who was telling me how he had mastered his anger problem. In the past, he had been prone to fits of rage and would often lose his temper with his wife. But now, he told me, he had everything under control. He had installed a "heavy bag" in his basement, and when he felt anger welling up inside him he would go down into the basement and punch the bag until he wasn't angry anymore. Sometimes, he admitted, he imagined that the punching bag was his wife.

My fear is that many of us adopt a slightly less terrible version of this strategy for dealing with our anger. When we feel rage, bitterness, and irritability building up inside us, we find a way to control it or expel it or calm it. But we never really deal with the problem.

But the good news that we read in James 4 is that God has a solution for our anger. According to verse 6, he "gives more grace." When you humble yourself before the Lord, he will meet you and supply all your needs. The solution to your anger is not to minimize or manage it; instead, you need to see it for how ugly it is. The Lord has given you a spouse so that you can love them the way that he loves his people. But instead, your overwhelming desire to get what you want makes you willing to go to war with them.

When you see how ugly your anger is, especially in light of the incredible kindness God has shown to you in Christ, it should be natural for you to "be wretched and mourn and weep." And when you come to God in brokenhearted humility over your sinful anger, you can be sure that he will be gracious to you in Christ. He forgives his people and helps them in their time of need. He will surely lift you up if you will come to him on your knees.

Next time you feel sinful anger welling up inside you, try to identify what you want so badly. Ask yourself, How am I being tempted to make an idol of this desire? How could I be willing to rage against my spouse simply in order to get what I want? And then resist the devil and submit yourself to God. You don't need to fight for whatever it is that you want. It is better to be wronged than to sin in your anger. And besides, God will give you everything that you truly need. Instead, let your anger drive you to God in repentance, for he gives grace to the humble.

Reflect: What kinds of conflicts do you and your fiancé typically have? Can you identify the desires that lie underneath those quarrels?

Act: If anger is a highway that leads to destruction, humble repentance is an off-ramp that leads us to God. Create a plan for how you will remind yourself to take that exit when you are tempted to give in to your anger.

DAY 30

Forgiveness and the Imitation of God

Let all bitterness and wrath and anger and clamor and slander be put away from you, along with all malice. Be kind to one another, tenderhearted, forgiving one another, as God in Christ forgave you. (Eph. 4:31–32)

I WONDER IF you realize what you've done. If you are reading this book, you may well have given someone a ring and asked them to marry you. If not, you probably accepted a ring and agreed to marry someone. In any event, I wouldn't be doing my job if I didn't point out that the person you are planning to marry is (wait for it) . . . a *sinner.*

In all seriousness, we have been looking at the ways that sin affects marriages and also ways in which God uses marriage to help us to be less sinful. And because you and your fiancé are sinners, you will need to give and receive forgiveness from each other.

My lovely wife and I have been married for a couple of decades now. We are both serious Christians. We are each other's best friends. We each treat the other well, and we love each other very much. But even so, we have had to ask each other's forgiveness time and time again over the years.

That might sound really basic—too simple to mention, in fact. But in my experience, most difficult marriages are not struggling to implement advanced, high-level marriage techniques (whatever those might be). Instead, most marriages struggle because spouses find it difficult to do things that seem basic, such as forgiving each other.

Make no mistake—forgiveness is difficult. When you forgive someone, you are releasing them—agreeing not to hold their offense against them anymore. In doing so, you are essentially agreeing to bear the cost of their sin rather than forcing them to bear it. That can feel very costly; it is often very difficult to forgive.

But forgiveness is not optional. In today's passage, Paul tells the church in Ephesus to forgive one another. Jesus tells his people to forgive each other relentlessly (see Matt. 18:21–22). In fact, he says that if we are not willing to forgive, then we should not expect the Father to forgive us either (see Matt. 6:15).

Hopefully you can see how this fits into the two big themes that we have been exploring.

Marriage is meant to be a picture of what God is like. And what does God do when the people whom he loves sin against him? He forgives. And so what does he want us to do when we are sinned against? He wants us to forgive.

The gospel is the key to living together in a Christian marriage. How do we learn to forgive? How do we cultivate the softness of heart that makes us willing to forgive those who sin against us? By reflecting on the cross of Christ. Jesus took the cost of our sin upon himself so that we could be completely forgiven. Our sins have been thrown into the depths of the sea (see Mic. 7:19). If someone has experienced that grace and mercy, they cannot help but extend that same mercy to others.

Reflect: Have you had an experience in which someone has truly forgiven you? How did it feel?

Act: Read the parable that Jesus tells in Matthew 18:21–35. Take time to pray, asking God to help you to forgive in the way that you have been forgiven.

DAY 31

Inviting Jesus to Your Wedding

So, whether you eat or drink, or whatever you do,
do all to the glory of God. (1 Cor. 10:31)

I WENT TO a wedding a couple of weeks ago. In many ways it was a lovely day—the venue was beautiful, the weather was perfect, the bride was radiant, the couple's love for each other was evident. It was a joyous day; you could feel the guests' happiness as they ate and enjoyed one another's company late into the night. It's just a shame that the couple didn't invite Jesus to the ceremony. I think he would have really enjoyed it.

As we conclude our time together, let's talk for a minute about your wedding ceremony. It could well be that a significant percentage of your mental and emotional bandwidth is currently being used to plan your wedding. That's fine; there's nothing wrong with that. And while the nature and quality of your ceremony does not have much (if any) impact on your life together, your wedding is important and worth doing well. And by "well," I mean "to the glory of God" (1 Cor. 10:31).

If you will allow me to be blunt (after all, we have been friends for a whole month now, right?), many wedding ceremonies are designed as if to help everyone to worship the bride and groom. Their great love for each other is held up as exemplary and worthy of joy. Poems are read, tributes are given, well-wishes are offered. But God gets only a cursory mention—if he gets even that.

Marriage is all about God. It is a display of his character and goodness—a living picture of Christ's gospel love for his people. The best weddings are not those that primarily celebrate the bride and groom but those that celebrate the good news of Jesus Christ and all that this means for his people.

Let me offer four suggestions that may help to make your wedding glorifying to God.

Pray. Pray for your wedding ceremony—not only that the weather would be good and that the details would go off without a hitch (though those are good things to pray for), but also that God would be glorified. Pray for guests who may not know Jesus—and especially that they would come to know him through your wedding.

Make sure that the gospel message is clear in your ceremony. There will probably be people present who do not know Jesus and do not have an opportunity to regularly hear about God's love for them in Christ. Make sure that the person who officiates at your wedding is able and willing to present the gospel in a compelling way.

Worship God in your ceremony. Sing God's praises together; pray together; hear from God's Word together. Make it clear to everyone through your planning who it is who is being glorified.

Be Christlike in everything. A wedding is a special occasion in a person's life, but it is not a license to be ill-tempered, selfish, demanding, or vain. While it is okay that other people are helping you and taking care of you on your big day, as a follower of Jesus you will always find your greatest happiness in being the servant of other people's joy.

As we have seen in this devotional, marriage isn't ultimately about us; it's about the glory of God. The wedding ceremony is no different!

Reflect: Think about the weddings you have been to. What things about them seemed to honor God? What things might take a ceremony's focus off God?

Act: If you haven't done so already, make a plan for a Christ-exalting wedding. Take time to pray with your fiancé about the ceremony.

Conclusion

THERE ARE SOME things that you can learn only by living through them. Karen and I have been married for a couple of decades now, and two things are for certain: I'm a better husband than I was back in 1997, and I'm nowhere near the husband I should be. If the Lord allows me more decades, I trust that I'll become much more loving, godly, and wise than I am now. And I trust that as I experience Karen's love for me, I'll have a better sense of God's love.

Now that we have reached the end of this little devotional, I pray that it has been helpful to you. But as we conclude, I am acutely aware of how much more there is to say and learn about marriage. It is impossible to do justice in thirty-one short readings to all the things you will need to know and discover over the course of your marriage. For that, you will need a church—friends, pastors, and older people who can mentor you along the way. And you will need to simply get on with the business of being married—with patience, forgiveness, hope, and love for each other.

My hope is that this book has served you by helping you with a few ideas and concepts—some raw materials that you can fashion into a God-glorifying marriage as you go along. Tips on communication and the differences between men and women can be helpful, but if they merely make us better at getting the things that we want from our spouses, I'm not sure they are what we need most. Every marriage will benefit most from the knowledge that God wants to use marriage to make us holy and to help us understand his love. With that realization in place, we can glorify God in the times of joy and the times of sorrow—in times when our spouses seem like a wonderful gift and times when we wonder if we would have been better off staying single.

I hope that God blesses your marriage with every joy—with companionship, children, laughter, and romance. When he does, make sure to thank him. Nothing in this life is better. And when difficulties come—conflict, financial pressures, children, health problems—realize that those things also come from your Father's loving hand. They are gifts too—ones that are meant to help us to grow and look more like Jesus. It's my prayer that your marriage will be a shining testimony to God's character and a beautiful picture of Christ's love for his bride until he comes.

God bless you.

Acknowledgments

I AM DEEPLY grateful to my lovely wife, Karen, for all of her love, encouragement, and support through the years. Throughout the process of writing this book I have been reminded of her kindness, gentleness, and patience over the course of our marriage. It goes without saying that this book wouldn't be possible without her.

I have looked up to Deepak Reju since we were both students at the George Washington University in the late 1990s. It's a joy to have a friend as an editor, and I am thankful for his invitation to me to write this book and for his assistance with its content. I am also glad that I managed to complete the manuscript before the Lord called one or both of us home. For a while, it wasn't looking likely.

I also must joyfully acknowledge the kind support of the Sterling Park Baptist Church. The congregation, and especially its elders, are relentlessly encouraging and accommodating. It's a joy to serve the Lord with you all.

Suggested Resources
for the Journey

Henderson, John. *Catching Foxes: A Gospel-Guided Journey to Marriage*. Phillipsburg, NJ: P&R Publishing, 2018. [If you are looking for material for premarital counseling, this book is theological, thoughtful, and practical. It will help you to build solid foundations for your upcoming marriage.]

Keller, Timothy, with Kathy Keller. *The Meaning of Marriage: Facing the Complexities of Commitment with the Wisdom of God*. New York: Dutton, 2011. [This book is biblical, practical, and insightful. It is a great introduction to and argument for God's design for marriage and how married couples ought to live it out together.]

Newheiser, Jim. *Marriage, Divorce, and Remarriage: Critical Questions and Answers*. Phillipsburg, NJ: P&R Publishing, 2017. [You've got questions; this book has answers! Its examination of forty common questions about every topic from dating to divorce makes it a great resource for pastors and counselors. It will also be useful for any Christian who wants to think through the Bible's teaching.]

Ortlund, Ray. *Marriage and the Mystery of the Gospel*. Wheaton, IL: Crossway, 2016. [A gem of a book. It is focused more on the story of the Bible than on the day-to-day practicalities of being married. But it rewards readers with a wonderful, hope-giving overview of God's purpose for marriage.]

Tripp, Paul David. *What Did You Expect? Redeeming the Realities of Marriage*. Wheaton, IL: Crossway, 2010. [Read this book when you are frustrated with your spouse. Better yet, read it right before you become frustrated with your spouse! It is a helpful reminder that the difficulties of marriage are all part of God's redemptive plan. You'll be encouraged, reassured, and challenged.]

BIBLICAL
COUNSELING
COALITION

The Biblical Counseling Coalition (BCC) is passionate about enhancing and advancing biblical counseling globally. We accomplish this through broadcasting, connecting, and collaborating.

Broadcasting promotes gospel-centered biblical counseling ministries and resources to bring hope and healing to hurting people around the world. We promote biblical counseling in a number of ways: through our 15:14 podcast, website (biblicalcounselingcoalition.org), partner ministry, conference attendance, and personal relationships.

Connecting biblical counselors and biblical counseling ministries is a central component of the BCC. The BCC was founded by leaders in the biblical counseling movement who saw the need for and the power behind building a strong global network of biblical counselors. We introduce individuals and ministries to one another to establish gospel-centered relationships.

Collaboration is the natural outgrowth of our connecting efforts. We truly believe that biblical counselors and ministries can accomplish more by working together. The BCC Confessional Statement, which is a clear and comprehensive definition of biblical counseling, was created through the cooperative effort of over thirty leading biblical counselors. The BCC has also published a three-part series of multi-contributor works that bring theological wisdom and practical expertise to pastors, church leaders, counseling practitioners, and students. Each year we are able to facilitate the production of numerous resources, including books, articles, videos, audio resources, and a host of other helps for biblical counselors. Working together allows us to provide robust resources and develop best practices in biblical counseling so that we can hone the ministry of soul care in the church.

To learn more about the BCC, visit biblicalcounselingcoalition.org.

More Marriage Resources
from P&R Publishing

Wayne Mack's classic marriage counseling resource uses thoughtful self-examination to reveal the personalities, backgrounds, and expectations that you and your future spouse are bringing to your union. Through rigorous Bible study, you will learn about God's expectations for marriage and be equipped with his solutions for dealing with typical marriage conflicts. Three follow-up lessons after your wedding help you to reflect on all that happens after you say, "I do."

For better or for worse? Whichever term describes your marriage, there are ways to make it (even) better. That's because God has designed marriage to be a relationship of deep unity and strength.

Wayne A. Mack recognizes the challenges before us and shows us how to meet those challenges with growing success. In this book, he has gathered a wealth of biblical insight and practical information on marital roles, communication, finances, sex, child-rearing, and family worship. Both as a counseling aid and as a guide for husbands and wives to study together, this book offers true hope and help where couples need it most.

Was this book helpful to you?
Consider writing a review online.
The author appreciates your feedback!

Or write to P&R at editorial@prpbooks.com
with your comments. We'd love to hear from you.